W9-DCJ-255

SONGS OF LIGHT

Selections from the Psalms

Published in Nashville, Tennessee, by Thomas Nelson, Inc.
and distributed in Canada by Lawson Falle, Ltd., Cambridge,
Ontario.

Text selections followed by the initials JB are by Jill Briscoe.
Text selections followed by the initials SB are by Stuart Briscoe.

Printed in Singapore by Tien Wah Press (pte.) Ltd.

ISBN 0-8407-4153-7

SONGS OF LIGHT

Selections from the Psalms in the New King James Version

Text by
Jill and Stuart Briscoe

Thomas Nelson Publishers
Nashville • Camden • New York

*Cause me to hear Your lovingkindness
in the morning, for in You do I trust.
Cause me to know the way
in which I should walk,
for I lift up my soul to You.*

Happy is he
who has the God of Jacob
for his help,
whose hope is in the Lord his God,
who made heaven and earth,
the sea, and all that is in them,
who keeps truth forever.

Look to the Lord

Unto You I lift up my eyes,
O You who dwell in the heavens.
Behold, as the eyes of servants look to
the hand of their masters,
as the eyes of a maid to the hand of
her mistress,
so our eyes look to the LORD our God,
until He has mercy on us.
Have mercy on us, O LORD,
have mercy on us!
For we are exceedingly filled with contempt.
Our soul is exceedingly filled
with the scorn of those who are at ease,
with the contempt of the proud.

*It is not easy to keep my eyes on You, Lord,
because there are so many things to distract me,
like being ridiculed and treated with contempt.
But You suffered these things more than I will
ever know, so I can learn from You how to
respond. But I will need to keep my eyes on
You.—SB*

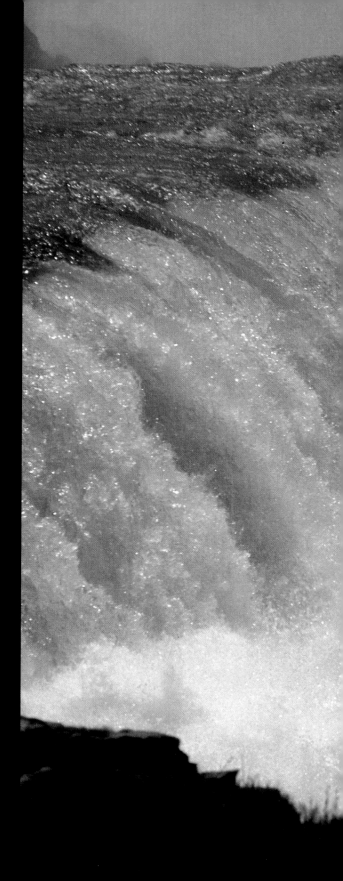

The Snare Has Been Broken

"If it had not been the LORD who was
on our side,"
let Israel now say—
"If it had not been the LORD who was
on our side,
when men rose up against us,
then they would have swallowed us alive,
when their wrath was kindled against us;
then the waters would have
overwhelmed us,
the stream would have gone over our soul;
then the swollen waters
would have gone over our soul."
Blessed be the LORD,
who has not given us as prey to their teeth.
Our soul has escaped as a bird from
the snare of the fowlers;
the snare is broken,
and we have escaped.
Our help is in the name of the LORD,
who made heaven and earth.

*Like a cork on a cataract, I feel that the
currents of life sweep me along. Like a bird
made to fly freely, I feel imprisoned by the bars
and chains of harsh circumstance. Without You,
Lord, I would be a victim of chance, a slave of
events, but You have freed me and proved to me
that I am a slave only to You. And there I find
my freedom.—SB*

The Lord Surrounds His People

Those who trust in the LORD
are like Mount Zion,
which cannot be moved,
but abides forever.
As the mountains surround Jerusalem,
so the LORD surrounds His people
from this time forth and forever.
For the scepter of wickedness shall not rest
on the land allotted to the righteous,
lest the righteous reach out their
hands to iniquity.
Do good, O LORD, to those who are good,
and to those who are upright in their hearts.
As for such as turn aside to their crooked ways,
the LORD shall lead them away
with the workers of iniquity.
Peace be upon Israel!

Hills that surround and protect the city of Jerusalem speak of a God who would have us trust His encircling care. Our fortress, our families, and even our faith can be shaken, yet we can choose a Mount-Zion-like quality of life so we shall not be moved.—JB

We Are Filled with Joy

When the LORD brought back the
captivity of Zion,
we were like those who dream.
Then our mouth was filled with laughter,
and our tongue with singing.
Then they said among the nations,
"The LORD has done great things for them."
The LORD has done great things for us,
whereof we are glad.
Bring back our captivity, O LORD,
as the streams in the South.
Those who sow in tears
shall reap in joy.
He who continually goes forth weeping,
bearing seed for sowing,
shall doubtless come again with rejoicing,
bringing his sheaves with him.

*Tears are not always tragic things. They can
drench the seeds of despair, teaching us hard
lessons of life from the dark days of experience.
Trouble grows us up to realize reality and to
reject triviality. Sowing seeds of truth in
faithless hearts can cause us to weep, too—but
wait a while—summer is coming and then we
will reap the harvest of happiness.—JB*

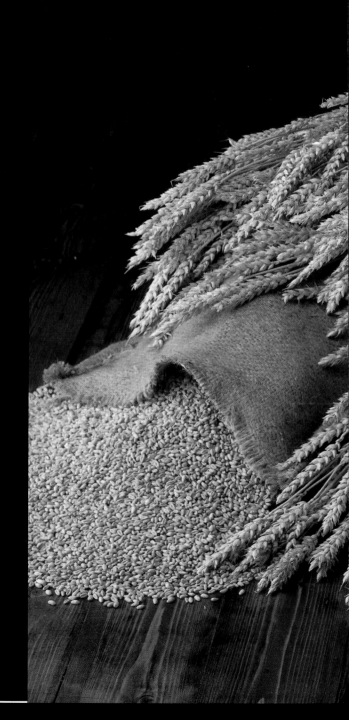

Children Are a Heritage

Unless the LORD builds the house,
they labor in vain who build it;
unless the LORD guards the city,
the watchman stays awake in vain.
It is vain for you to rise up early,
to sit up late,
to eat the bread of sorrows;
for so He gives His beloved sleep.
Behold, children are a heritage from
the LORD,
the fruit of the womb is His reward.
Like arrows in the hand of a warrior,
so are the children of one's youth.
Happy is the man who has his quiver
full of them;
they shall not be ashamed,
but shall speak with their enemies in
the gate.

We are a race of achievers, Lord, and I suppose You made us that way. But we have become overly impressed by our achievements and under impressed by our inadequacies; we need to be reminded of our limitations. Every time I look at a child it is as if You are saying, "Go on, man, make one of those!" Then I remember how little I can do without You.—SB

Like a Fruitful Vine

Blessed is every one who
fears the LORD,
who walks in His ways.
When you eat the labor of your hands,
you shall be happy,
and it shall be well with you.
Your wife shall be like a fruitful vine
in the very heart of your house,
your children like olive plants
all around your table.
Behold, thus shall the man be blessed
who fears the LORD.
The LORD bless you out of Zion,
and may you see the good of
Jerusalem all the days of your life.
Yes, may you see your children's children.

"Fruitful vines" and "olive shoots" are not the expressions I usually employ to describe my wife and children, Lord. But to the psalmist they spoke of special blessings, and I certainly agree with his sentiments. How can I thank You enough for those whom You have brought into my life to bless and to cheer, to encourage and support? I suppose the only way to thank You is to treat them as You would wish, and that I will do as You enable me.—SB

But the Lord Is Righteous

"Many a time they have afflicted
me from my youth,"
let Israel now say—
"Many a time they have afflicted me
from my youth;
yet they have not prevailed against me.
The plowers plowed on my back;
they made their furrows long."
The LORD is righteous;
He has cut in pieces the cords of the wicked.
Let all those who hate Zion
be put to shame and turned back.
Let them be as the grass on the housetops,
which withers before it grows up,
with which the reaper does not fill his hand,
nor he who binds sheaves, his arms.
Neither let those who pass by them say,
"The blessing of the LORD be upon you;
we bless you in the name of the LORD!"

*To have only bitter memories of your youth can
color the present gray and the future black.
Knowing God can cause you to use your somber
background to paint the canvas of your mind
with the bright colors of forgiveness. Painting
pictures like that will make people who are
hateful take notice of Your faith.*—JB

Unto You I lift up my eyes,
O You who dwell in the heavens.

More Than Watchmen Wait for the Morning

Out of the depths I have cried to You,
O LORD;
LORD, hear my voice!
Let Your ears be attentive
to the voice of my supplications.
If You, LORD, should mark iniquities,
O LORD, who could stand?
But there is forgiveness with You,
that You may be feared.
I wait for the LORD, my soul waits,
and in His word I do hope.
My soul waits for the LORD
more than those who watch for the morning—
I say, more than those who watch for the morning.
O Israel, hope in the LORD;
for with the LORD there is mercy,
and with Him is abundant redemption.
And He shall redeem Israel
from all his iniquities.

*God does not keep a running record of my
wrongs. He does not keep books! I am glad! I
can expect His love to help me do the same.
Blame blights the blessing of prayer. I must not
blame God. After all—once I am forgiven—He
does not blame me!—*JB

Like a Weaned Child with Its Mother

LORD, my heart is not haughty,
nor my eyes lofty.
Neither do I concern myself with
great matters,
nor with things too profound for me.
Surely I have calmed and quieted my soul,
like a weaned child with his mother;
like a weaned child is my soul within me.
O Israel, hope in the LORD
from this time forth and forever.

It is hard to be humble, Lord, but it is harder to be proud. The psalmist discovered this and so did I. In the end we have to learn to trust, to rest in You. It stands to reason we must, but unfortunately we are not always reasonable. So keep doing what is necessary to teach us what is necessary—to trust and obey.—SB

This Is My Resting Place Forever and Ever

Lord, remember David
and all his afflictions;
how he swore to the Lord,
and vowed to the Mighty God of Jacob:
"Surely I will not go into the chamber of my house,
or go up to the comfort of my bed;
I will not give sleep to my eyes or
slumber to my eyelids,
until I find a place for the Lord,
a dwelling place for the Mighty God of Jacob."
Behold, we heard of it in Ephrathah;
we found it in the fields of the woods.
Let us go into His tabernacle;
let us worship at His footstool.
Arise, O Lord, to Your resting place,
You and the ark of Your strength.
Let Your priests be clothed with righteousness,
and let Your saints shout for you.
For Your servant David's sake,
do not turn away the face of Your Anointed.
The Lord has sworn in truth to David;
He will not turn from it:
"I will set upon your throne the fruit of your body.
If your sons will keep My covenant
and My testimony which I shall teach them,
their sons also shall sit upon your throne forevermore."
For the Lord has chosen Zion;
He has desired it for His habitation:
"This is My resting place forever;
here I will dwell, for I have desired it.
I will abundantly bless her provision;
I will satisfy her poor with bread.
I will also clothe her priests with salvation,
and her saints shall shout aloud for joy.
There I will make the horn of David grow;
I will prepare a lamp for My Anointed.
His enemies I will clothe with shame,
but upon Himself His crown shall flourish."

*David had the idea for a temple but You would
not let him build it, Lord. You allowed Solomon
to build it and he was overcome with the
thought that You would inhabit a building
made with hands. Now You live in Your church.
Give us David's desire to build the body and
Solomon's wonder that You actually inhabit
it.—SB*

When Brothers Live in Unity

Behold, how good and how pleasant it is
for brethren to dwell together in unity!
It is like the precious oil upon the head,
running down on the beard,
the beard of Aaron,
running down on the edge of his garments.
It is like the dew of Hermon,
descending upon the mountains of Zion;
for there the LORD commanded the blessing—
life forevermore.

Unity that allows diversity, with Christian forbearance and tolerance, is like the dew of Mount Hermon. It comes from God and keeps friendships fragrant and fresh. It is beautiful—and possible—when you know Jesus!—JB

Minister by Night

**Behold, bless the Lord,
all you servants of the Lord,
who by night stand in the house
of the Lord!
Lift up your hands in the sanctuary,
and bless the Lord.
The Lord who made heaven and earth
bless you from Zion!**

*The shortest of the Psalms talks of
ministering through the longest of
nights. Some of the Levites were
charged with this holy watch. It was
a night duty that involved praising
God in the dark. When God charges
any of us with such a duty—may we
be found faithful!*—JB

His Treasured Possession

Praise the LORD!
Praise the name of the LORD;
praise Him, oh you servants of the LORD!
You who stand in the house of the LORD,
in the courts of the house of our God,
praise the LORD, for the LORD is good;
sing praises to His name,
for it is pleasant.
For the LORD has chosen Jacob for Himself,
Israel for His special treasure.
For I know that the LORD is great,
and our LORD is above all gods.
Whatever the LORD pleases He does,
in heaven and in earth,
in the seas and in all deep places.
He causes the vapors to ascend from
the ends of the earth;
He makes lightning for the rain;
He brings the wind out of His treasuries....
Your name, O LORD, endures forever,
Your fame, O LORD, throughout all generations.
For the LORD will judge His people,
and He will have compassion on His servants.
The idols of the nations are silver and gold,
the work of men's hands.
They have mouths, but they do not speak;
eyes they have, but they do not see;
they have ears, but they do not hear;
nor is there any breath in their mouths.
Those who make them are like them;
so is everyone who trusts in them.
Bless the LORD, O house of Israel!
Bless the LORD, O house of Aaron!
Bless the LORD, O house of Levi!
You who fear the LORD,
bless the LORD!
Blessed be the LORD out of Zion,
who dwells in Jerusalem!
Praise the LORD!

*You chose Jacob, Lord, and made him into
Israel. It was a long, arduous procedure, but
You worked as slowly and relentlessly as the
waves beating on the beaches. From the
beginning he was precious to You, Lord, and in
this I find comfort, for I, too, need a lot of
work and I know You will do it, for I am
precious to You, too.—SB*

His Love Endures Forever

Oh, give thanks to the LORD,
for He is good!
For His mercy endures forever.
Oh, give thanks to the God of gods!
For His mercy endures forever.
Oh, give thanks to the LORD of lords!
For His mercy endures forever:
to Him who alone does great wonders,
for His mercy endures forever;
to Him who by wisdom made the heavens,
for His mercy endures forever;
the moon and stars to rule by night,
for His mercy endures forever.
to Him who struck Egypt in their firstborn,
for His mercy endures forever;
and brought out Israel from among them,
for His mercy endures forever.

If that old seat could speak, Lord, it would tell of young lovers gazing at the moon with stars in their eyes. And it would tell of those same lovers torn by tragedy, exchanging tears for stars. But through the changing seasons of life, You are the unchanging lover, for Your love endures through eternity. And that puts a sparkle in all our eyes.—SB

Those who sow in tears shall reap in joy.

He Led His People

With a strong hand,
and with an outstretched arm,
for His mercy endures forever;
To Him who divided the Red Sea in two,
for His mercy endures forever;
And made Israel pass through
the midst of it,
for His mercy endures forever;
But overthrew Pharaoh and his army
in the Red Sea,
for His mercy endures forever;
To Him who led His people through
the wilderness,
for His mercy endures forever;
To Him who struck down great kings,
for His mercy endures forever;
And slew famous kings,
for His mercy endures forever—
Sihon king of the Amorites,
for His mercy endures forever;
And Og king of Bashan,
for His mercy endures forever—
And gave their land as a heritage,
for His mercy endures forever;
A heritage to Israel His servant,
for His mercy endures forever.
Who remembered us in our lowly state,
for His mercy endures forever;
And rescued us from our enemies,
for His mercy endures forever;
Who gives food to all flesh,
for His mercy endures forever.
Oh, give thanks to the God of heaven!
for His mercy endures forever.

*"His mercy endures forever." God's
people have and always will rely on
His faithfulness. In the Old
Testament, grace proceeded law.
God's lovingkindness was proved by
His constant care. We must count
our blessings or we will forget all He
has done for us.—JB*

How Can We Sing in a Foreign Land?

By the rivers of Babylon,
there we sat down, yea, we wept
when we remembered Zion.
We hung our harps
upon the willows in the midst of it.
For there those who carried us away
captive required
of us a song,
and those who plundered us required of us
mirth,
saying, "Sing us one of the songs
of Zion!"
How shall we sing the LORD's song
in a foreign land?
If I forget you, O Jerusalem,
let my right hand forget her skill!
If I do not remember you,
let my tongue cling to the roof
of my mouth—
if I do not exalt Jerusalem
above my chief joy.
Remember, O LORD, against the sons of
Edom the day of Jerusalem,
who said, "Raze it, raze it,
to its very foundation!"
O daughter of Babylon,
who are to be destroyed,
happy shall he be who repays you as you
have served us!
Happy shall he be who takes and dashes
your little ones against the rock.

The children of Israel had hung up their harps on a weeping willow tree. They were sung out. Have we also hung up our joy on a "grief" tree, a "gripe" tree, or even a "grade" tree? The Babylonians demanded a song from believers. Unbelievers should hear one from us. Perhaps it will be in a minor key, but then, who says a song in a minor key is not beautiful!—JB

The Lord Will Fulfill His Purpose

I will praise You with my whole heart;
before the gods I will sing praises to You.
I will worship toward Your holy temple,
and praise Your name
for Your lovingkindness and Your truth;
for You have magnified Your word
above all Your name.
In the day when I cried out,
You answered me,
and made me bold with strength in my soul.
All the kings of the earth shall praise
You, O LORD,
when they hear the words of Your mouth.
Yes, they shall sing of the ways
of the LORD,
for great is the glory of the LORD.
Though the LORD is on high,
yet He regards the lowly;
but the proud He knows from afar.
Though I walk in the midst of trouble,
You will revive me;
You will stretch out Your hand
against the wrath of my enemies,
and Your right hand will save me.
The LORD will perfect that which
concerns me;
Your mercy, O LORD, endures forever;
do not forsake the works of Your hands.

Sometimes I feel like a tiny boat on the endless expanse of the seas. My mind drifts across the waters to the continents, and I think of You in charge of them all. It is hard to believe that with all the universe on Your mind You have me there, too. But You say You do and I believe You. So I'll bend my back to my tasks and trust You to fill them with purpose.—SB

You Know Me, O Lord

O LORD, You have searched me
and known me.
You know my sitting down
and my rising up;
You understand my thought afar off.
You comprehend my path
and my lying down,
and are acquainted with all my ways.
For there is not a word on my tongue,
but behold, O LORD,
You know it altogether.
You have hedged me behind and before,
and laid Your hand upon me.
Such knowledge is too wonderful for me;
it is high, I cannot attain it.
Where can I go from Your Spirit?
Or where can I flee from Your presence?
If I ascend into heaven, You are there;
if I make my bed in hell, behold,
You are there.
If I take the wings of the morning,
and dwell in the uttermost parts of the sea,
even there Your hand shall lead me,
and Your right hand shall hold me.
If I say, "Surely the darkness shall
fall on me,"
even the night shall be light about me;
indeed, the darkness shall not hide from You,
but the night shines as the day;
the darkness and the light are both
alike to You.

*I know You know me, Lord, and this knowledge
fills me with joy because knowing me as You
do, You love me just the same. But it troubles
me that knowing You as I do I still try to hide
and run away—exercises in futility and insult.
But one thing heartens me and it is this: one
day I will know You as I am known and then I
will want only You. Till then, hold me close,
Lord.—SB*

How Precious
Are Your Thoughts

For You have formed my inward parts;
You have covered me in my mother's womb.
I will praise You, for I am fearfully
and wonderfully made;
marvelous are Your works,
and that my soul knows very well.
My frame was not hidden from You,
when I was made in secret,
and skillfully wrought in the lowest
parts of the earth.
Your eyes saw my substance,
being yet unformed.
And in Your book they all were written,
the days fashioned for me,
when as yet there were none of them.
How precious also are Your thoughts
to me, O God!
How great is the sum of them!
If I should count them, they would be
more in number than the sand;
when I awake, I am still with You.
Oh, that You would slay the wicked,
O God!
Depart from me, therefore, you bloodthirsty men.
For they speak against You wickedly;
Your enemies take Your name in vain.
Do I not hate them, O Lord, who hate You?
And do I not loathe those who rise up
against You?
I hate them with perfect hatred;
I count them my enemies.
Search me, O God, and know my heart;
try me, and know my anxieties;
and see if there is any wicked way in me,
and lead me in the way everlasting.

*We are fearfully and wonderfully made. We
must stand still and understand God's total
knowledge of us, worshiping Him for it. We
need to stop running into the maze of ourselves.
Then we will find we are thoroughly
known—and can be content.* —sb

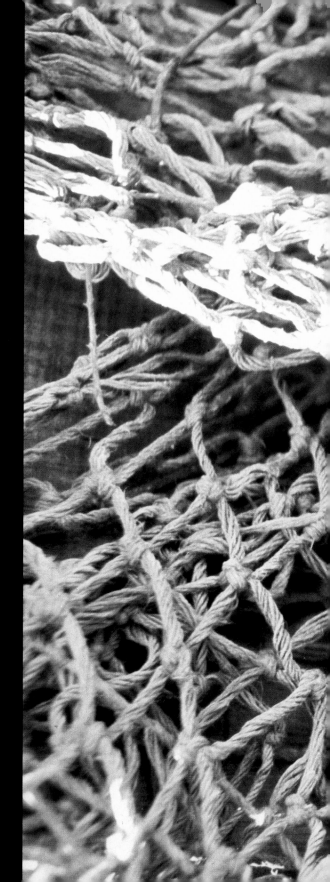

The Lord Secures Justice

Deliver me, O Lᴏʀᴅ, from evil men;
preserve me from violent men,
who plan evil things in their hearts;
they continually gather together for war.
They sharpen their tongues like a serpent;
the poison of asps is under their lips.　　Selah
Keep me, O Lᴏʀᴅ, from the hands of
the wicked;
preserve me from violent men,
who have purposed to make my steps stumble.
The proud have hidden a snare for me, and cords;
they have spread a net by the wayside;
they have set traps for me.　　Selah
I said to the Lᴏʀᴅ: "You are my God;
hear the voice of my supplications, O Lᴏʀᴅ.
O God the Lᴏʀᴅ, the strength of my salvation,
You have covered my head in the day of battle.
Do not grant, O Lᴏʀᴅ, the desires of the wicked;
do not further his wicked scheme,
lest they be exalted.　　Selah
"As for the head of those who surround me,
let the evil of their lips cover them;
let burning coals fall upon them;
let them be cast into the fire,
into deep pits, that they rise not up again.
Let not a slanderer be established in the earth;
let evil hunt the violent man to overthrow him."
I know that the Lᴏʀᴅ will maintain
the cause of the afflicted, and justice for the poor.
Surely the righteous shall give thanks
to Your name;
the upright shall dwell in Your presence.

*Misused men and women can in turn mistreat
others. This practice is called "revenge."
Redemption takes vengeance to the cross and
cancels it out. God turns hatred into a
dedicated desire to change a cruel world. We
need to pray for mangled souls; God will hear
and answer. He understands.—*SB

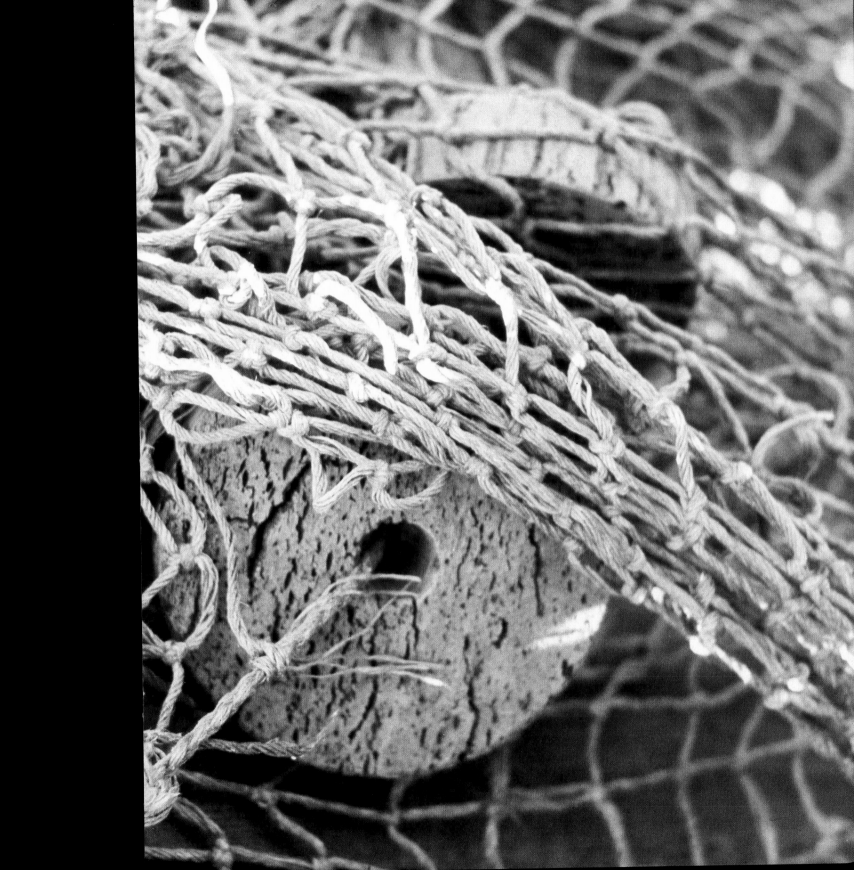

Come Quickly to Me

Lord, I cry out to You; make haste to me!
Give ear to my voice when I cry out to You.
Let my prayer be set before You as incense,
the lifting up of my hands as the
evening sacrifice.
Set a guard, O Lord, over my mouth;
keep watch over the door of my lips.
Do not incline my heart to any evil thing,
to practice wicked works
with men who work iniquity;
and do not let me eat of their delicacies.
Let the righteous strike me;
it shall be a kindness.
And let him reprove me;
it shall be as excellent oil;
let my head not refuse it.
For still my prayer is against the deeds
of the wicked.
Their judges are overthrown by the
sides of the cliff,
and they hear my words,
for they are sweet.
Our bones are scattered at the mouth
of the grave,
as when one plows and breaks up the earth.
But my eyes are upon You,
O God the Lord;
in You I take refuge;
do not leave my soul destitute.
Keep me from the snares which they
have laid for me,
and from the traps of the workers of iniquity.
Let the wicked fall into their own nets,
while I escape safely.

*My lips are inadequate, my best expressions
inarticulate, but sometimes my hands speak
with eloquence. See them lifted high, Lord and
read the yearning of my heart to lay hold of
You. They are empty hands, Lord; I have
nothing to give that is not already Yours. My
hands are open, Lord, where once they were
clenched in selfish grasping and they are ready
to do Your bidding.—SB*

*How precious are
your thoughts to me, O God!
How great is the sum of them!
If I should count them,
they would be more in number
than the sand.*

I Tell the Lord My Trouble

I cry out to the LORD with my voice;
with my voice to the LORD I make my
supplication.
I pour out my complaint before Him;
I declare before Him my trouble.
When my spirit was overwhelmed within
me, then You knew my path.
In the way in which I walk
they have secretly set a snare for me.
Look on my right hand and see,
for there is no one who acknowledges me;
refuge has failed me;
no one cares for my soul.
I cried out to You, O LORD:
I said, "You are my refuge,
my portion in the land of the living.
Attend to my cry,
for I am brought very low;
deliver me from my persecutors,
for they are stronger than I.
Bring my soul out of prison,
that I may praise Your name;
the righteous shall surround me,
for You shall deal bountifully with me."

*The prettiest path is strewn with
leaves that died. The brightest light
casts shadows on the way. Life is
not without its dark side; people
flourish and fade, aspirations are
born and die. But in the midst of it
all I will tell the Lord my trouble.
This refreshes me for the next step of
the way, round the corner, into the
unknown tomorrow.—SB*

I Hide Myself in You

Hear my prayer, O LORD,
give ear to my supplications!
In Your faithfulness answer me,
and in Your righteousness.
Do not enter into judgment with Your servant,
for in Your sight no one living is righteous.
For the enemy has persecuted my soul;
he has crushed my life to the ground;
he has made me dwell in darkness,
like those who have long been dead.
Therefore my spirit is overwhelmed within me;
my heart within me is distressed.
I remember the days of old;
I meditate on all Your works;
I muse on the work of Your hands.
I spread out my hands to You;
my soul longs for You like a thirsty
land.   Selah
Answer me speedily, O LORD;
my spirit fails!
Do not hide Your face from me,
lest I be like those who go down into the pit.
Cause me to hear Your lovingkindness
in the morning, for in You do I trust;
cause me to know the way in which I should walk,
for I lift up my soul to You.
Deliver me, O LORD, from my enemies;
in You I take shelter.
Teach me to do your will,
for You are my God; your Spirit is good.
Lead me in the land of uprightness.
Revive me, O LORD, for Your name's sake!
For Your righteousness' sake bring my
soul out of trouble.
In Your mercy cut off my enemies,
and destroy all those who afflict my soul;
for I am Your servant.

God gave memories to His people to encourage them. Through difficult times, God's spirit will bring to our remembrance His words which will lead us to level ground. Then we shall avoid the potholes of spiritual poverty. Remembering in the night results in rejoicing in the morning.—SB

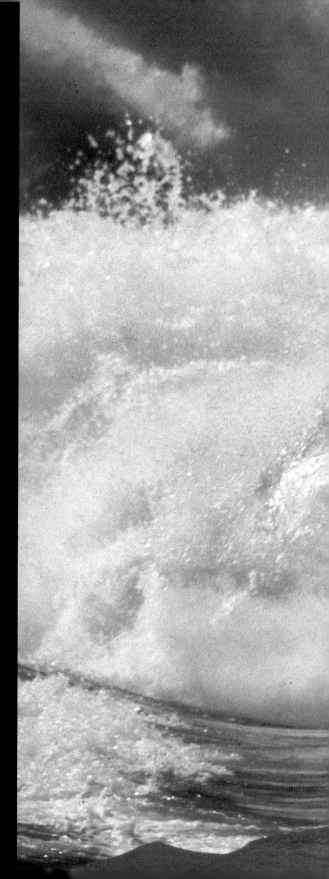

Blessed Are the Lord's People

Blessed be the LORD my Rock,
who trains my hands for war,
and my fingers for battle—
my lovingkindness and my fortress,
my high tower and my deliverer,
my shield and the One in whom I take refuge,
who subdues my people under me.
LORD, what is man,
that You take knowledge of him?
Or the son of man,
that You are mindful of him?
Man is like a breath;
his days are like a passing shadow.
Bow down Your heavens, O LORD,
and come down; touch the mountains,
and they shall smoke.
Flash forth lightning and scatter them;
shoot out Your arrows and destroy them.
Stretch out Your hand from above;
rescue me and deliver me out of great waters,
from the hand of foreigners,
whose mouth speaks vain words,
and whose right hand is a right hand of falsehood.
I will sing a new song to You, O God;...
the One who gives salvation to kings,
who delivers David His servant from the deadly sword.
Rescue me and deliver me from the hand of foreigners,
whose mouth speaks vain words,
and whose right hand is a right hand of falsehood—
that our sons may be as plants grown up in their youth;
that our daughters may be as pillars,
sculptured in palace style;
that our barns may be full,
supplying all kinds of produce;
that our sheep may bring forth thousands
and ten thousands in our fields;
that our oxen may be well-laden;
that there be no breaking in or going out;
that there be no outcry in our streets.
Happy are the people who are in such a state;
happy are the people whose God is the LORD!

*Everyone wants a safe world for his or her
children to live in. David certainly did.
Sometimes a war has to be fought to make our
world secure. At other times, prosperity and
peace reign and everyone is happy. Both in
times of war and of peace, we need to remember
humbly that God is in control.*—JB

They Will Celebrate Your Goodness

I will extol You, my God, O King;
and I will bless Your name forever and ever.
Every day I will bless You,
and I will praise Your name forever and ever.
Great is the LORD,
and greatly to be praised;
and His greatness is unsearchable.
One generation shall praise Your works to another,
and shall declare Your mighty acts.
I will meditate on the glorious splendor of Your majesty,
and on Your wondrous works.
Men shall speak of the might of Your awesome acts,
and I will declare Your greatness.
They shall utter the memory of Your great goodness,
and shall sing of Your righteousness.
The LORD is gracious and full of compassion,
slow to anger and great in mercy.
The LORD is good to all,
and His tender mercies are over all His works.
All Your works shall praise You, O LORD,
and Your saints shall bless You.
They shall speak of the glory of Your kingdom,
and talk of Your power,
to make known to the sons of men
His mighty acts,
and the glorious majesty of His kingdom.

You are good, Lord, and everything You have made is, according to Your own evaluation, good, too. It was good of You to entrust Your good works to us for our enjoyment and employment. But what we have done is not good. We have abused Your creation and spurned Your salvation. Have mercy on us, Lord, for truly You are good.—SB

You Open Your Hand

Your kingdom is an everlasting kingdom,
and Your dominion endures throughout all generations.
The LORD upholds all who fall,
and raises up all those who are bowed down.
The eyes of all look expectantly to You,
and You give them their food in due season.
You open Your hand and satisfy the desire of every
living thing.
The LORD is righteous in all His ways,
gracious in all His works.
The LORD is near to all who call upon Him,
to all who call upon Him in truth.
He will fulfill the desire of those who fear Him;
He also will hear their cry and save them.
The LORD preserves all who love Him,
but all the wicked He will destroy.
My mouth shall speak the praise of the LORD,
and all flesh shall bless His holy name forever and ever.

*Your open-handedness contrasts starkly with my
tight-fistedness, Lord. You give of Yourself and
Your creation for the benefit of mankind, but I
have a tendency to take and keep. You offer
freely from Your resources and I gladly accept,
often forgetting to share. And when, like a
wounded chick, I run to You, I find such
comfort in Your strong gentleness that I am able
to comfort those who are hurting around me.
Teach me the secret of the open hand.—SB*

He Upholds the Cause of the Oppressed

Praise the LORD!
Praise the LORD, O my soul!
While I live I will praise the LORD;
I will sing praises to my God while I
have my being.
Do not put your trust in princes,
nor in a son of man,
in whom there is no help.
His spirit departs,
he returns to his earth;
in that very day his plans perish.
Happy is he who has the God of Jacob
for his help,
whose hope is in the LORD his God,
who made heaven and earth,
the sea, and all that is in them;
who keeps truth forever,
who executes justice for the oppressed,
who gives food to the hungry.
The LORD gives freedom to the prisoners.
The LORD opens the eyes of the blind;
the LORD raises those who are bowed down;
the LORD loves the righteous.
The LORD watches over the strangers;
He relieves the fatherless and widow;
but the way of the wicked He turns upside down.
The LORD shall reign forever—
your God, O Zion, to all generations.
Praise the LORD!

It is hard to trust God when we are hungry or hurt. It is so much easier to trust fellow humans, which is dangerous because we are only little "dust" people who return to the ground when we die. God never disintegrates. He promises to put our lives back together again. We can trust him.—JB

He Grants Peace to Your Borders

Praise the LORD!
For it is good to sing praises to our God;
for it is pleasant, and praise is beautiful.
The LORD builds up Jerusalem;
He gathers together the outcasts of Israel.
He heals the broken-hearted
and binds up their wounds.
He counts the number of the stars;
He calls them all by name.
Great is our LORD, and mighty in power;
His understanding is infinite.
The LORD lifts up the humble;
He casts the wicked down to the ground.
Sing to the LORD with thanksgiving;
sing praises on the harp to our God,
He does not delight in the strength of the horse;
He takes no pleasure in the legs of a man.
The LORD takes pleasure
in those who fear Him,
in those who hope in His mercy.
Praise the LORD, O Jerusalem!
Praise your God, O Zion!
For He has strengthened the bars of your gates;
He has blessed your children within you.
He makes peace in your borders,
and fills you with the finest wheat.
He sends out His command to the earth;
His word runs very swiftly.
He gives snow like wool;
He scatters the frost like ashes;
He casts out His hail like morsels;
who can stand before His cold?
He sends out His word and melts them;
He causes His wind to blow,
and the waters flow.
He declares His word to Jacob,
His statutes and His judgments to Israel.
He has not dealt thus with any nation;
and as for His judgments,
they have not known them.
Praise the LORD!

Broken hearts take time to heal. We can fill the hours with a song while we wait. God is so busy I am amazed He has time to listen to music. But He does—especially the music of faith. —JB

The eyes of all
look expectantly to You,
and You give them
their food in due season.
You open Your hand and
satisfy the desire
of every living thing.

The People Close to His Heart Praise Him

Praise the LORD!
Praise the LORD from the heavens;
praise Him in the heights!
Praise Him, all His angels;
praise Him, all His hosts!
Praise Him, sun and moon;
praise Him, all you stars of light!
Praise Him, you heavens of heavens,
and you waters above the heavens!
Let them praise the name of the LORD,
for He commanded and they were created.
He has also established them forever and ever;
He has made a decree which shall not pass away.
Praise the LORD from the earth,
you great sea creatures and all the depths;
fire and hail, snow and clouds;
stormy wind, fulfilling His word;
mountains and all hills;
fruitful trees and all cedars;
beasts and all cattle;
creeping things and flying fowl;
kings of the earth and all peoples;
princes and all judges of the earth;
both young men and maidens; old men and children.
Let them praise the name of the LORD,
for His name alone is exalted;
His glory is above the earth and heaven.
and He has exalted the horn of His people,
the praise of all His saints—
of the children of Israel, a people near to Him.
Praise the LORD!

You, Lord, are a God of vastness. Wide horizons and views of space give me an awed impression of Your magnitude. It would be easy to live in dread of Your greatness, paralyzed by my smallness, but You knew this and revealed Your closeness. I have learned with all Your people that You are nearer than breathing, for You gave me the living Christ. For this I praise You.—SB

The Glory of All His Saints

Praise the LORD!
Sing to the LORD a new song, and His
praise in the congregation of saints.
Let Israel rejoice in their Maker;
Let the children of Zion be joyful
in their King.
Let them praise His name with the dance;
Let them sing praises to Him with the
timbrel and harp.
For the LORD takes pleasure in His people;
He will beautify the humble
with salvation.
Let the saints be joyful in glory;
Let them sing aloud on their beds.
Let the high praises of God
be in their mouth,
And a two-edged sword in their hand,
To execute vengeance on the nations,
And punishments on the peoples;
To bind their kings with chains,
And their nobles with fetters of iron;
To execute on them the written judgment—
This honor have all His saints.
Praise the LORD!

In many ways I feel like clay in the
potter's hands, without any
significance until molded into
something of Your designing, Lord.
What a thrill to know that I have
been made by You! And yet, this
thought shows I am far more
valuable than clay, for clay cannot
think. More than that, clay cannot
appreciate being a pot, so it cannot
thank the potter. But I can and do
and will. I praise You, Lord.—SB

Let Everything Praise the Lord

Praise the LORD!
Praise God in His sanctuary;
praise Him in His mighty firmament!
Praise Him for His mighty acts;
praise Him according to His excellent greatness!
Praise Him with the sound of the trumpet;
praise Him with the lute and harp!
Praise Him with the timbrel and dance;
praise Him with stringed instruments and flutes!
Praise Him with loud cymbals;
praise Him with high sounding cymbals!
Let everything that has breath praise the LORD.
Praise the LORD!

*Praise appreciates God. It reminds us He is
worth everything. Praise helps us realize who
He is so we can understand who we are and be
glad about it. Being appreciative is something
God appreciates from us!—JB*

Lord, what is man,
that You take knowledge of him?
Or the son of man,
that you are mindful of him?
Man is like a breath;
his days are like
a passing shadow.

Oh, give thanks to the Lord,
for He is good!
Oh, give thanks
to the God of gods!
Oh, give thanks
to the Lord of lords!